Intentional Marriage
The Art of Loving Your Husband

Crystal Brothers

Intentional Marriage: The Art of Loving Your Husband

Copyright © 2014 by Crystal Brothers

ISBN-13: 978-1495247118
ISBN-10: 1495247112

DEDICATION

To my loving husband, Chad Brothers. Words can't express the blessing you are to me every day, just by being you. Thank you for your unwavering support and faith in me.

Contents

Introduction

"Little children, let us not love in word or talk but in deed and in truth."
1 John 3:18

The biggest threat to marriages in our modern world is daily neglect. When we stop trying, we start drifting apart.

We get caught up in the busyness of life.

We get selfish.

We get thoughtless.

We get prideful and entitled and start to focus on the ways our husband isn't doing this or that...or maybe he *is* doing this or that annoying thing.

Slowly, one day at a time, we can reach a crisis point in our marriage, just by {not} doing the small things.

If you are at that crisis point of your marriage, take heart. With God's help, nothing is hopeless. And you *can* improve yourself and improve your marriage.

This book is based on a simple concept. There is a saying attributed to Gandhi, "You must be the change you want to see in the world."

The words are true, and I believe they apply to marriage as well. This book is written for wives. Not because I believe that all of the problems in your marriage are your fault. But the fact of the matter is that focusing on your husband's faults breeds discontentment, and it isn't productive. You cannot nag, pout, argue, or complain enough to change your husband. What you *can* do, though, is change yourself.

Not so long ago, I found myself in one of those bad places. I was focusing on my husband's faults and my needs, when it should have been the opposite. Through this challenge, an amazing thing happened. I started waking up asking myself, "What can I do to bless my husband today?"

It's a painfully simple concept but one that radically changed my life and marriage.

Notice I said it *radically changed my life*. Even though this was a marriage challenge, the change went beyond my marriage. My walk with God was strengthened as I sought to honor Him through my marriage and my actions toward my husband.

The even more amazing thing is that the change that took place in me changed my husband. When I started submitting to him, serving him, and intentionally loving him, he responded to me in completely different ways. As the testimonies started coming in from other women who were joining me in the challenge, I found I wasn't alone in this. Wives were changed, husbands were changed, and marriages were strengthened.

It is my prayer that you will experience that change in your life as you commit to honoring God in your marriage. I have prayed for you, dear reader, in every step of the writing process.

Because I realize we are all busy, I did not want this book to be one more burdensome thing for you. I have intentionally kept the daily readings brief. This challenge is not about the readings; it's about the action.

The idea is simply that you do something intentional to love your husband every single day for the next 31 days.

And then? Don't stop. Keep it going. Keep looking for little ways to bless your husband every single day.

And you know what? I'm guessing you'll be blessed, as well. Probably in ways you won't even expect, because that tends to happen when we selflessly love others.

Crystal Brothers

Day 1: Praise Your Husband, Avoid Criticism

"Death and life are in the power of the tongue,
and those who love it will eat its fruits."
Proverbs 18:21a

Today's challenge is to use your tongue to lift up your husband, to create *life* in him instead of death. This principle is simple, and yet, the practice is not so easy at times. Find something about your husband for which you can honestly praise him. Seek out positive words that you can speak to him.

At the same time, resist the urge to criticize or speak negative things to him. You might be surprised at the effect such a simple change can have on the overall tone of your home.

What was the hardest thing about today's challenge? Did this reveal anything in your heart that needs to change? Pray that the Lord will show you how you can become more like Him.

_____

_____

_____

_____

_____

_____

_____

_____

_____

_____

_____

_____

_____

_____

Day 2: Greet Your Husband

"A glad heart makes a cheerful face,
but by sorrow of heart the spirit is crushed."
Proverbs 15:13

Greet your spouse with a smile when he comes home from work (or when you come home from work, depending on your personal situation).

So often the stress of the day leads me to greet my husband in less than attractive ways. Sometimes, he comes home from a long, stressful day at work, and I greet him by immediately unloading all of the stressful things about *my* day.

Home should be a refuge, a sanctuary. One of the ways that I can give that to my husband is by making an effort to greet him with a smile after a long day. That's not to say we can't talk about the day, but I should let him catch his breath before I start unloading on him.

Today's challenge is to greet your husband cheerfully when he comes home from work. Start your evening off on a more positive note.

How did it feel to begin your evening on a more positive note? Did you notice a difference in your evening or in your own attitude?

_____

_____

_____

_____

_____

_____

_____

_____

_____

_____

_____

_____

_____

_____

Day 3: Serve Your Husband

"...even as the Son of Man came not to be served but to serve, and to give his life as a ransom for many."
Matthew 20:28

Women who choose to honor and serve their husbands are often called doormats. I see this very differently. If serving, rather than being served, was good enough for my Lord and Savior, then I'm okay with it!

Today's challenge is a bit vague, because we all have different husbands and different situations. Do something above and beyond your typical work to serve your husband. If you always wash dishes, do laundry, and cook, then those do not count. Do something above and beyond. Is there something you let go that particularly bothers your husband? Fix it if you can. Since our families are all different, this challenge will look different for different people.

For me, this challenge was cleaning out our van. We tend to accumulate kid-related items in there, and it drives my husband a little crazy.

What can you do for your husband today?

What did you do to serve your husband today? What was his reaction?

(PS—if his reaction wasn't what you hoped, don't focus on feelings here. He may not have noticed. He may not have said anything about it. But *you* did a good thing, and the Lord notices. Never forget that!)

_____

_____

_____

_____

_____

_____

_____

_____

_____

_____

_____

_____

_____

Day 4: Cook Your Husband's Favorite Food

"Better is a dinner of herbs where love is than a fattened ox and hatred with it."
Proverbs 15:17

Yikes! I've never hated my husband, but I guarantee there have been times when he would have preferred a smaller meal served with love and joy instead of a great meal that is served with a hateful attitude.

Don't make your hubby choose between a good meal and a loving wife—give him both! They say that the way to a man's heart is through his stomach.

Today's challenge is to fix your hubby's favorite meal (or pie, cookies, breads, fried chicken) for dinner.

How did it feel to make your husband's favorite meal or dessert? Were you able to do so with a willing and cheerful heart?

_____

_____

_____

_____

_____

_____

_____

_____

_____

_____

_____

_____

_____

Day 5: Do Something Fun With Your Husband

"Then he said to them, 'Go your way. Eat the fat and drink sweet wine and send portions to anyone who has nothing ready, for this day is holy to our Lord. And do not be grieved, for the joy of the LORD is your strength.'"
Nehemiah 8:10

The joy of the Lord is strength in our lives, and I believe joy is strength for our marriage as well.

Have some FUN with your husband today! Watch something you enjoy on TV, play a game together, or go for a walk. The specifics don't matter. Just do something together that you can both enjoy.

Sometimes in the busyness of life (and parenting), spending fun quality time together falls by the wayside. Today's challenge is to take some time to do something fun with your husband.

What did you do for today's challenge? Do you routinely spend time enjoying your husband's company? If not, what are the barriers to this, and what can you do to overcome them?

Don't focus on the problems. Focus on one solution. Focus on one thing you can do to increase your quality time with your husband.

_____

_____

_____

_____

_____

_____

_____

_____

_____

_____

_____

_____

_____

Day 6: Pray With and for Your Husband

"Therefore, confess your sins to one another and pray for one another, that you may be healed. The prayer of a righteous person has great power as it is working."
James 5:16

I'll be bold and say this challenge is something we should be doing every single day. But, again, it's something that we need to be intentional about. We have to make prayer a non-negotiable priority.

Today's challenge is to pray with and for your spouse today. If you already do this consistently (great job!), then take it to the next level–pray with him, pray more often, or ask him what specific things he needs prayer for.

Also, don't forget the power of praying God's word! Do that for your husband today.

Did you ask your husband about his specific needs today? What did you pray for your husband today? How can you make this a daily priority for your marriage?

Day 7: Give Your Husband Grace

"And as you wish that others would do to you, do so to them."
Luke 6:31

I know that you've all heard this verse before. But did you know that it's right in the midst of a bunch of verses about loving even those who wrong you? I challenge you to read the verse in context.

I chose this verse because most of us want grace extended to us. (I don't know many people who criticize the police officer for *not* writing that speeding ticket they deserved!) However, we are slow to give it to others.

Today's challenge is to bestow grace to your husband. Maybe he does something you don't like. Perhaps he leaves his dirty clothes lying about or is thoughtless about those special holidays. Maybe he is short-tempered with you. (I'm not talking about abuse here. There is a difference!) Whatever it is, give him grace today instead of sharp words.

How does it affect your day when someone extends grace to you? How can you be more grace-filled when responding to your husband? How could it change your marriage for the better if you choose to respond with grace?

_____

_____

_____

_____

_____

_____

_____

_____

_____

_____

_____

_____

_____

_____

Day 8: 5 things You Love About Your Husband

"Therefore encourage one another and build one another up, just as you are doing."
1 Thessalonians 5:11

Too often, we spend our time and our words criticizing and tearing down our husbands instead of building them up. But the Bible calls us to encourage one another as Christians. How much more should we encourage and build up our husbands?

Today's challenge is to make it a point to encourage your husband.

Make a list of 5 things you love about him or a list of 5 things that he does well. Too often, we take our spouses for granted. Either give him the list or tell him those things throughout the day today. Build him up!

What 5 things did you use to encourage your husband with today?
What keeps you from praising him and building him up more often?
How might your relationship change if you were to be more
intentional about this?

_____

_____

_____

_____

_____

_____

_____

_____

_____

_____

_____

_____

Day 9: Improve as a Companion and as a Helper

"Then the LORD *God said, 'It is not good that the man should be alone; I will make him a helper fit for him.'"*
Genesis 2:18

We are told in Genesis that God created Eve as a helper and companion for Adam. Today's challenge focuses on a tough question—are you a good companion for your husband?

Today's challenge is to pray about ways that you can improve yourself or your actions to better fill your role as helper and companion to your husband. Pray about it, think about it, and, if you're really brave, just ask him. Ask him how you can better fulfill this God-given role. (But only if you're not going to get mad at him for answering--don't set him up!) And start to implement at least one of those changes today.

I don't see this role as being a slave to him, but, rather, it is a role of helping and supporting him—mostly just basic, common sense courtesies that get forgotten over time. Give him those courtesies again.

What are 3 things you can improve on in order to be a better companion and a better helper? What steps can you immediately take to better fill this role? How might your marriage and yourself improve if you work harder at this?

_____
_____
_____
_____
_____
_____
_____
_____
_____
_____
_____
_____
_____
_____

Day 10: Send Your Husband an Encouraging Verse

"All Scripture is breathed out by God and profitable for teaching, for reproof, for correction, and for training in righteousness, that the man of God may be complete, equipped for every good work."
2 Timothy 3:16-17

God's word is alive, and it has the power to be exactly what we need it to be at any given moment. Does your husband need encouragement today? Is he stressed about work? Does he need to know how much God loves him? Or maybe he has a favorite verse that speaks life to him and reminds him of the goodness and glory of God.

Today's challenge is to spend some time in the scriptures, pray about it, and find something that will speak to your husband's heart. Send it to him through an email, text, Facebook message, handwritten note, or voicemail.

Use God's word to speak *life* to him today.

What verse did you send your husband? Is it a favorite of his? How can you use God's word to speak life to your husband more often?

_____

_____

_____

_____

_____

_____

_____

_____

_____

_____

_____

_____

Day 11: Date Night!

"For where your treasure is, there your heart will be also."
Matthew 6:21

It is so important for us to honor our spoken priorities with actions. Most of us would probably say that our marriage is important to us. God first, then marriage, children, and so on.

But do your time and resources spent reflect that? Do you spend time with your husband, intentionally building your relationship? When my husband and I were engaged, a wise friend told us that he and his wife always had a weekly date night. For more than 40 years, they made it a priority to set aside some time each week to spend with one another.

It was long before we'd heard of such a thing, but his words made sense, so we've made that a priority so far in over 8 years of marriage. We now live away from family, so it's a little more difficult. But not impossible, and my marriage is worth the effort. My husband is worth the effort.

Today's challenge is to spend some time with your husband. Have a date night. Can't go out? Then do it at home. Get creative. (See the Bonus files for some great at-home date night ideas.)

What was the best part of your "date" together? How can you make dating your husband a priority? How might your marriage be affected if you become more intentional about time together?

_____
_____
_____
_____
_____
_____
_____
_____
_____
_____
_____
_____
_____
_____

Day 12: Focus on Forgiveness

"Put on then, as God's chosen ones, holy and beloved, compassionate hearts, kindness, humility, meekness, and patience, bearing with one another and, if one has a complaint against another, forgiving each other; as the Lord has forgiven you, so you also must forgive."
Colossians 3:12-13

Sometimes, our husbands just know how to push our buttons. We live with them, and when you put all that "flesh" and "sin" together, it's not going to be pretty. Sometimes we will clash. Disagreements and arguments are going to happen.

But when it gets scary, when it starts leading down a very bad path, we tend to let those things take root in our hearts as bitterness and resentment. That is essentially when we stop forgiving.

Ruth Bell Graham said, "A happy marriage is a union of two forgivers."

Today's challenge might be tough. Use today to focus on forgiveness. Is there something that you are holding against your husband? Something that is in the past that gets brought up at every argument? Or some past hurt that you're holding onto?

Today's challenge is to start letting that go. Confess that you are holding a grudge, and ask God to help you give it over to Him.

Forgive your husband as the Lord forgave you.

Do you tend to hold onto past hurts or offenses? Is there anything in your heart causing bitterness? How can you avoid falling into this trap in the future?

_____

_____

_____

_____

_____

_____

_____

_____

_____

_____

_____

_____

_____

_____

Day 13: A Day of Rest

"Remember the Sabbath day, to keep it holy. Six days you shall labor, and do all your work, but the seventh day is a Sabbath to the LORD your God. On it you shall not do any work, ... For in six days the LORD made heaven and earth, the sea, and all that is in them, and rested on the seventh day. Therefore the LORD blessed the Sabbath day and made it holy."
Exodus 20:8-11

You might be wondering what this has to do with marriage.

When we don't listen to our bodies (and the Lord) and take that time of rest, everything we do is affected by it. We become grumpy, short-tempered, cranky, and we aren't as effective as wives, mothers, or people.

If you're anything like me, your husband is probably the first person to feel the effects when you start to push your boundaries and take on too much.

Today's challenge is to honor the Sabbath by allowing yourself to rest. The truth is, when you take the time to rest, the "working" time will be more efficient and probably more enjoyable for everyone.

Do you find it difficult to "turn off" and take that time of rest? What do you notice about yourself when you do make rest a priority? What are some steps you can take to add more margin to your life and day, allowing yourself more rest?

_____

_____

_____

_____

_____

_____

_____

_____

_____

_____

_____

_____

_____

_____

Day 14: Look Out for His Interests

"Do nothing from selfish ambition or conceit, but in humility count others more significant than yourselves. Let each of you look not only to his own interests, but also to the interests of others."
Philippians 2:3-4

It's so easy for us to become selfish. It is in our sinful nature to focus on our wants and needs above everything else. But Paul calls us to have a mind like Christ and put the interests of others above our own. I believe this is especially necessary in marriage. Selfishness and self-centeredness are the opposite of love, and they have no place in our marriages.

Today's challenge is to focus on your husband's needs. Give him some time for himself when he comes home from work today. Allow him to relax in peace by watching TV, tinkering in the garage, having time with friends, or by relaxing in whatever way that he chooses. Do it cheerfully, not begrudgingly.

Pray that God will help you to sincerely want the best for your husband.

Was it difficult for you to generously allow your husband that time? How can you be more selfless in order to focus on his needs more than your own? What are some specific steps you can take now?

Day 15: Thank God for Him

"I thank my God in all my remembrance of you,"
Philippians 1:3

Having an "attitude of gratitude" is so important. It is truly amazing how much that attitude can affect every aspect of your life. Are you truly thankful for your husband?

So often, we choose to focus on the negative things--those little nit-picky things that drive us crazy. Sometimes, we can get in a funk with our attitude and marriage so that, instead of giving thanks to God every time we think of our husband, we focus and stew on the negative things.

Today's challenge is to give thanks for your husband every time you think of him. Having an attitude of thanks will change your actions toward him.

Did you find it difficult to truly give thanks for your husband every time you thought of him? How might your actions change if you challenge yourself to cultivate gratitude for your husband?

_____

_____

_____

_____

_____

_____

_____

_____

_____

_____

_____

_____

_____

_____

_____

Day 16: Be His Support

"Two are better than one, because they have a good reward for their toil. For if they fall, one will lift up his fellow. But woe to him who is alone when he falls and has not another to lift him up! Again, if two lie together, they keep warm, but how can one keep warm alone? And though a man might prevail against one who is alone, two will withstand him—a threefold cord is not quickly broken."
Ecclesiastes 4:9-12

This passage reminds us of some of the ways that a friend can offer support. As wives, we should be all of this and more to our husbands. My husband needs to know that I will be there to help him up when he falls, to keep him warm, to help defend him.

Instead, I'm sad to say that there are times I have heaped guilt, frustration, and nagging on him when I should have offered support and understanding. There are times when I have compounded his problems instead of making them better.

Today's challenge is to commit to being that support for your husband. Be the one who makes life easier for him; be the one who helps him when he needs it. Resist the urge to criticize him when he's down. Maybe this issue won't come up today. But file it away for the next time your husband makes a mistake or is feeling discouraged.

Have you ever criticized when your husband needed love and support? How can you make sure to be the one who helps him instead of hinders him?

_____

_____

_____

_____

_____

_____

_____

_____

_____

_____

_____

_____

_____

Day 17: Flirt with Him

*"Many waters cannot quench love, neither can floods drown it.
If a man offered for love all the wealth of his house,
he would be utterly despised."*
Song of Solomon 8:7

Many waters cannot quench love...and neither can time, parenthood, financial worries, or the like. But, the thing is, sometimes, we have to fight for it.

In Song of Solomon, we read about a fresh, new, on-fire kind of love. Probably the kind most of us had when we were dating our husbands. We longed to spend time with him, we flirted with him, and we looked our best for him. My, how things change over the years! But they don't have to. We can still pursue our husbands, and we should.

Today's challenge is to flirt with your husband. Smile for him, laugh with him, do all those little things you did in the beginning to win his heart.

What little things did you do today to flirt with your husband? If it seemed awkward, how can you make it a normal part of your day? What effect do you think it could have on your marriage if you make it a priority?

_____

_____

_____

_____

_____

_____

_____

_____

_____

_____

_____

_____

_____

_____

Day 18: Fix Yourself Up

"Behold, you are beautiful, my love, behold, you are beautiful! Your eyes are doves behind your veil. Your hair is like a flock of goats leaping down the slopes of Gilead."
Song of Solomon 4:1

Saying someone has hair like a flock of goats doesn't sound very much like a compliment these days. But for Solomon, it demonstrates that he was very much in love with this woman and was in awe of her beauty. The most important thing for us is to note that she had put effort into pleasing him with her appearance.

I know this is a delicate topic, so I want to be clear. I believe that husbands should love their wives unconditionally, period. However, I think we wives owe it to our husbands to try a little harder. Most of us fix ourselves up at least a little to go out of the house or to meet up with girlfriends. Our husbands are more important than any of that, and they deserve some effort from us. As a stay-at-home mom, it's all too easy for me to fall into that sweats, ponytail, no make-up rut. But working women can fall into this as well. You dress up every day for work and may not feel like doing it at home.

Today's challenge is to spend a few minutes fixing yourself up. Just 5-8 minutes to put on some real clothes, brush your hair, and dust on some make up or something. Show him that he is worth your effort.

How did it make you feel to put some effort into your appearance? Does making an effort with your appearance affect your confidence or motivation?

Day 19: Do Not be Conformed

"Do not be conformed to this world, but be transformed by the renewal of your mind, that by testing you may discern what is the will of God, what is good and acceptable and perfect."
Romans 12:2

Marriage is one of the things that has been most corrupted by this world. Where God's word says we should submit to our husbands, society says that women should rebel against them to be "real women." Where God's word says we should respect our husbands, society says women should laugh at and make fun of them. Where God's word says that He hates divorce, the world says that we should focus on our own happiness and leave if we get tired of trying.

Today's challenge is to go to the source. Dig into God's word. Get a concordance or search a site like Biblegateway.com and find what God's word says about love and marriage. Find what He calls wives to do.

Look up and read at least 5 verses pertaining to marriage and loving our husbands. Once we see to what He has called us, we need to let His word transform us and no longer be conformed to this world. We are called to be set apart.

Are there any values you have been taught that are contrary to God's word? Which verses did you read? Will they be easy or difficult to follow?

_____

_____

_____

_____

_____

_____

_____

_____

_____

_____

_____

_____

_____

_____

Day 20: Get to Know Your Husband's Heart

"But the LORD said to Samuel, 'Do not look on his appearance or on the height of his stature, because I have rejected him. For the LORD sees not as man sees: man looks on the outward appearance, but the LORD looks on the heart.'"

1 Samuel 16:7

God looks at our hearts. The Bible also tells us that LOVE covers a multitude of sins. I believe these concepts go hand in hand. Understanding nurtures compassion. When I can see my husband's heart and trust in what I know about him, it's easier for my love to cover those sins and misunderstandings. It makes me more willing to give him the benefit of the doubt and believe the best of him.

Today's challenge is to spend some time getting to know your husband–really talking and listening to him. Here are a few thought-provoking questions to start the conversation (see the bonus materials for more conversation starters).

1. What is your favorite book/verse of the Bible and why?
2. What is your biggest struggle in following God's will for your life? (Then pray!)
3. If you could go anywhere on vacation, where would it be?
4. If you could live anywhere, where would it be?
5. What incident in your childhood or adult life most shaped your faith?

Did you learn anything about your husband through your conversation today? How can you make it a priority to keep learning about him, even in the mundane?

Day 21: Give Him a Gift

"In all things I have shown you that by working hard in this way we must help the weak and remember the words of the Lord Jesus, how he himself said, 'It is more blessed to give than to receive.'"
Acts 20:35

We all like to get a random, just-because-I-love-you kind of surprise. I have received a few such surprises that have blessed me and turned around a bad day.

Today give your husband a gift. I know that finances are tight for a lot of us, but you can probably spare a couple of dollars for something small, even if it's just his favorite candy bar for a treat. If not, make him something. Be creative and be thoughtful. :)

Have fun thinking of something that will bless him and will let him know that you were thinking about him today.

What special thing did you give your husband? How can you make it a priority to bless him more often in the little things?

_____

_____

_____

_____

_____

_____

_____

_____

_____

_____

_____

_____

_____

_____

Day 22: Love is...

"Love is patient and kind; love does not envy or boast; it is not arrogant or rude. It does not insist on its own way; it is not irritable or resentful; it does not rejoice at wrongdoing, but rejoices with the truth. Love bears all things, believes all things, hopes all things, endures all things. Love never ends...."
1 Corinthians 13:4-8

If there is ever a doubt that you are treating your husband in a loving way, the verses above create a standard by which to measure yourself. This is what true love is and does.

Today's challenge is two-fold. First, if you haven't already memorized this passage, I want you to join me in fully memorizing it. Once it's there, be prepared for God to use it in chastening you, and allow these words to be a constant reminder of how you should treat your husband.

Secondly, choose one of these aspects of love to work on today. You know your husband and your relationship best, and you know specifically what your greatest need is.

Which aspect did you choose to focus on? Which aspects are strengths/weaknesses for you? How can you work toward living out these verses in your marriage?

_____

_____

_____

_____

_____

_____

_____

_____

_____

_____

_____

_____

_____

Day 23: Respect Him

"However, let each one of you love his wife as himself,
and let the wife see that she respects her husband."
Ephesians 5:33

Research has shown that, for the most part, women most need to feel loved while men most need to feel respected. The complex thing is that our men are all different and what makes them feel respected might be different as well. Some basic things might include: trusting his judgment and decisions, not speaking negatively about him to others, and not disagreeing with him openly in front of your children or other people.

Today's challenge is to respect your husband. And note in the verse above, there is no "if" or "unless." We are called to respect our husbands, period. I know that might be harder for some than for others. But I believe God knows best, and we can flourish and experience His joy and fulfillment most fully when we are following His will and directions.

What characteristics about yourself make respecting your husband difficult? How can you work on your own attitude and follow God's word in this more fully?

Day 24: Guard Your Heart

"Keep your heart with all vigilance, for from it flow the springs of life." Proverbs 4:23

Adultery might seem removed from a Christian's life, but the truth is that it is happening at an alarming rate within the church.

Such situations rarely happen all at once. It starts with one small, bad decision at a time. We must be intentional about guarding our hearts, in all aspects of our life and faith. But it's especially important when it comes to our marriages, where people so often "follow their hearts."

We must guard our hearts against emotional ties that aren't honoring to our husbands. Furthermore, we should guard our hearts from thoughts of discontent regarding our marriage and against any other way Satan can gain a foothold.

Today's challenge is to guard your heart against negativity and discontentment. When those negative thoughts creep in, counter them with something positive. Examine your relationships, especially with the opposite sex, and be sure that you are honoring your husband. If not, take steps to end any unhealthy relationships immediately.

Are you honoring your husband with your relationships, thoughts, and actions? Are you striving to guard your heart against negativity and discontent where your marriage is concerned?

_____

_____

_____

_____

_____

_____

_____

_____

_____

_____

_____

_____

_____

_____

Day 25: Speak Only What is Helpful

"Let no corrupting talk come out of your mouths, but only such as is good for building up, as fits the occasion, that it may give grace to those who hear."
Ephesians 4:29

This is one of those verses that always convicts me--both in my daily life and in marriage. Sometimes, I say things I shouldn't. A good filter for everything we say is to ask ourselves, "Is it helpful?" Is your comment going to build someone up or tear them down? Will it encourage your husband or discourage him? Will it make him feel loved or lacking?

Today's challenge is to judge your speech by this verse, especially toward your husband. Only speak what is edifying and beneficial to him.

Do you struggle with your words and tone toward your husband? How do you think your marriage would be affected if you filtered your words through this verse?

_____

_____

_____

_____

_____

_____

_____

_____

_____

_____

_____

_____

_____

_____

Day 26: Brag About Your Husband

"What is your beloved more than another beloved, O most beautiful among women? What is your beloved more than another beloved, that you thus adjure us?"
Song of Solomon 5:9

There is a disturbing trend I've noticed. Instead of counting our blessings, we spend our time having some sort of contest with other women about whose life is hardest. Have you noticed this? Sometimes the conversations center on our finances, to-do lists, or children. But sometimes, they center on our husbands.

We mention with disdain how "Susie is so lucky, and her life is so much easier because her husband has a better job." Or "Jane is so lucky, because her husband helps out with the children more." If our own husbands did that, we'd be happier. We want everyone to know how challenging our life is, so we stop counting our blessings. Instead, we want to win the pity-party battle.

In Song of Solomon, she had clearly been talking about how wonderful her beloved was, so much so that the other ladies challenged her, "What's so great about your beloved? Why is he better than the others?" And in verses 5:10-16, she answers them in flowery language, lifting up her beloved.

Today's challenge is to not be pulled in to that "woe is me" mentality. Instead, count your blessings. Give your husband the honor of lifting him up to other people instead of tearing him down. Yes, he has his faults. We all do. But don't let that be what you put on display for others to see.

How often do you build up your husband in the presence of others? When you talk about him with girlfriends, do you show his best side or his worst?

_____

_____

_____

_____

_____

_____

_____

_____

_____

_____

_____

_____

_____

_____

Day 27: Let Him Know You Find Him Attractive

"My beloved is radiant and ruddy, distinguished among ten thousand"
Song of Solomon 5:10

"His mouth is most sweet, and he is altogether desirable. This is my beloved and this is my friend,..."
Song of Solomon 5:16

Yesterday we talked about how the Shulamite girl was challenged to defend her man. This verse is a part of her response. We typically focus on women as needing to be encouraged about their appearance, but the same is true for men. He needs to know that you find him attractive, that you notice his manly strength, and all of that good stuff. Men have an innate need to be a protector. Let him know that you recognize that.

Reassure your husband.

Today's challenge is to let your husband know that you find him attractive. If possible, initiate a time of intimacy with him. It is so important that we cultivate that close relationship in our marriages.

Does your husband know that you find him attractive? What can you do to speak these words to him more often?

_____

_____

_____

_____

_____

_____

_____

_____

_____

_____

_____

_____

_____

_____

Day 28: Listen to Him

"Know this, my beloved brothers: let every person be quick to hear, slow to speak, slow to anger;"
James 1:19

I have a confession to make. Sometimes, I put words in my husband's mouth. I *think* I know what he's thinking or what he's going to say, and I react accordingly.

As I was reading this verse recently, the Lord led me to focus on the end of it: "...and slow to become angry." And it hit me—if I really did the first part of that verse, the second part might follow more naturally. Because if I really listened to my husband with no preconceived notions, no insecurities coloring what I think he is going to say, I might just get angry less.

Try it out today. This isn't just about those times of argument. Make sure that you aren't getting so bogged down by other responsibilities that you're too busy to engage your husband in conversation and listen to him.

Today's challenge is simple—talk less, listen more.

What are some things that make it difficult for you to really listen to and pay attention to your husband? How can you work toward removing, or working around, those obstacles? How might your marriage improve as your listening skills improve?

_____
_____
_____
_____
_____
_____
_____
_____
_____
_____
_____
_____
_____
_____

Day 29: Submit to Your Husband

"Wives, submit to your own husbands, as to the Lord. For the husband is the head of the wife even as Christ is the head of the church, his body, and is himself its Savior. Now as the church submits to Christ, so also wives should submit in everything to their husbands."
Ephesians 5:22-24

You probably knew it was coming. I don't think we could have a marriage challenge without it. Ephesians 5:22, the verse that causes so much contention in our modern society. We just don't like that verse. But it's there. And it's painfully clear. God calls us to submit to our husbands.

Although the call to submit to our husbands is clear, it might look differently for each couple. Sometimes submitting is about letting go of our way of doing things, and our expectations.

Today's challenge is two-fold: 1) search your heart and relationship and 2) take a step toward more fully submitting to your husband in some area.

Is it difficult for you to submit to your husband? What aspect is hardest to overcome, and how can you improve on it?

_____

_____

_____

_____

_____

_____

_____

_____

_____

_____

_____

_____

_____

Day 30: Assure Him of Your Devotion

"But Ruth said, 'Do not urge me to leave you or to return from following you. For where you go I will go, and where you lodge I will lodge. Your people shall be my people, and your God my God.'"
Ruth 1:16

I love this picture of devotion, love, and faithfulness that we see from Ruth toward her mother-in-law. It's a beautiful thing. Unfortunately in our society, it's increasingly uncommon. We don't see that kind of devotion in relationships very often, even in marriages.

Can your husband count on you to say this to him? Does he know that you are going to be by his side, come what may? Does he know that you will follow him to the ends of the earth, that you will love his people and call them your own (think in-laws for this one!)?

I know this passage isn't talking about a husband-wife relationship, but this kind of devotion should be a given in a husband-wife relationship.

Today's challenge is to remember all the things you promised your husband. Look back at your wedding vows. Are you living them out?

Does your husband know that he can count on you to live out these verses? What are some ways that you can help him feel more secure in your love and devotion to him and your marriage?

_____

_____

_____

_____

_____

_____

_____

_____

_____

_____

_____

_____

_____

_____

Day 31: Pursue Peace

"Turn away from evil and do good; seek peace and pursue it."
Psalm 34:14

Many arguments that we have with our husbands stem from a desire to be right. We want our needs and expectations to be met. We want things to be done our way. And, above all else, we want to be right. We want him to see (and agree with) our point of view. We refuse to give in and let things go.

But God's word says that we should seek peace *and* pursue it. It's important enough that it's one of those things we see twice. Once in Psalm 34:14 and then reiterated in 1 Peter 3:11 at the end of a passage about marriage.

Today's challenge is to be diligent in seeking peace and in pursuing it in your marriage. If an argument arises or if your husband does something you'd normally pounce on, just let it go.

Let it go.

Value peace above being right.

Do you find it difficult to let things go for the sake of peace? Pray that the Lord will move on your heart in this area.

Day 32: What Now?

*"No one has ever seen God; if we love one another,
God abides in us and his love is perfected in us."*
1 John 4:12

I know what you're probably thinking: the challenge is over. And you're right. The challenge was only 31 days. But I hope that was just a start. I hope it's not only about a 31 day challenge, but instead, that it is about a lasting heart change and revitalizing our marriages.

The verse above isn't really about marriage, but, again, I think it's shown most clearly in marriage. Paul talks about the parallel of the husband-wife relationship to Christ and His church. A strong marriage, a loving marriage, is such a wonderful, beautiful thing.

I pray that you will continue the challenge to study God's word and seek Him in your marriage and to do something intentional every day to bless your husband and strengthen your marriage. I certainly plan to continue to be intentional in my marriage. It's all too easy to get caught up in the busyness of life otherwise.

How can you continue this challenge and make it a lifelong habit instead of a month-long challenge? Make an action plan. What things can you commit to doing daily to pour into your husband and your marriage?

_____
_____
_____
_____
_____
_____
_____
_____
_____
_____
_____
_____

Resources

Crystal Brothers

101 Ways to Bless Your Husband

Need ideas for being intentional in your marriage? Here are 101 fun ideas to get you started.

Tip: Write some of these ideas onto slips of paper, along with some of your own. Fold up the strips and put them in a jar, and draw one out each morning to help you be intentional every day in your marriage.

1. Smile at him.
2. Let him know he's important to you.
3. Give him your full attention when he's talking.
4. Give him time to spend with friends.
5. Let go of the small stuff.
6. Watch his favorite TV show or movie with him.
7. Let him enjoy his hobbies and show interest in them.
8. Tell him how much you appreciate him.
9. Don't criticize him.

10. Laugh together.

11. Buy him a small, unexpected gift.

12. Plan a date night.

13. Write him a love note.

14. Make him breakfast in bed.

15. Greet him with a smile when he comes home from work.

16. Call him just to say "I love you."

17. Give him time to relax.

18. Only speak positive things about him to others.

19. Compliment his appearance.

20. Do small acts of service for him throughout the day.

21. Slow dance to "your song" in your living room.

22. Don't over-commit yourself. Leave time for him.

23. Give him grace.

24. Tell him and show him that you need him.

25. Admit when you're wrong and apologize.

26. Be patient with his mistakes.

27. Submit to him.

28. Support his pursuits and encourage him in his job.

29. Rub his feet or neck after a hard day.

30. Be interested in what interests him.

31. Fix his coffee in the morning.

32. Defend him if others criticize him.

33. Complete one of his chores for him.

34. Thank him for his hard work to provide for you.

35. Tell him why you're proud to be married to him.

36. If you need to confront something, do it lovingly.

37. Encourage leadership in him.

38. Initiate lovemaking.

39. Keep your expectations reasonable.

40. Make his favorite dessert.

41. Make it a point to notice and mention things he does for you.

42. Brag about him to others.

43. Give him space when he's tired or needs it.

44. List 5 things you love about him.

45. Surprise him with a gift card in his wallet for lunch out.

46. Wash his car and fill it up with gas.

47. Get up with him in the mornings.

48. Be his "help-mate."

49. Only disagree or argue in private.

50. Learn his love language.

51. If he's in a bad mood don't respond with grumpiness.

52. Show love to his relatives.

53. Go to bed at the same time at night.

54. Strive to serve him.

55. Don't compare him unfavorably to other men.

56. Fix his favorite meal.

57. Thank him for things he's done around the house.

58. Don't hold things over his head that you do.

59. Don't make big decisions without his support or input.

60. Let him sleep in on his day off.

61. Don't talk down to him, or insult him.

62. Don't turn him down sexually, save energy for him.

63. Let him enjoy an evening free of responsibilities.

Crystal Brothers

64.   Give him a clean house to come home to.

65.   Discover his sexual needs.

66.   Wink at him from across the room.

67.   Give him the benefit of the doubt.

68.   Wear his favorite outfit.

69.   Visit him at work, or take him a special treat there.

70.   Be kind to him. Don't treat other people better than you treat him.

71.   Don't blame him for things that aren't his fault.

72.   Don't say "I told you so."

73.   Put a note in his vehicle for him to find as he leaves for work.

74.   Surprise him with an overnight date.

75.   Hold his hand.

76.   Kiss him goodbye when he leaves for work.

77.   Tell him you love him more often.

78.   Surprise him with a treat or love note in his lunch box.

79.   Ask him what he'd like to do this evening.

80.   Don't expect him to read your mind.

81.   Give him time alone.

82.   Don't nag him.

83.   Look your best for him.

84.   Send him a sexy text message.

85.   Honor him—don't criticize him in front of others.

86.   Be his companion during a chore.

87.   Don't give him the silent treatment.

88.   Share a favorite Bible verse with him.

89.   Pray for him.

82

90. Don't whine or complain.

91. Thank God for him every time you think of him today. Tell him you did this.

92. Hide love notes around the house for him.

93. Don't undermine his authority in front of your children. Let them see you respect him.

94. Let him talk about his day and stress of his job.

95. Recognize and compliment his talents.

96. Write a love note to him on the bathroom mirror.

97. Give him couples coupons to redeem.

98. Honor Him.

99. Be his cheerleader.

100. Make a video of you and your children listing reasons you love him.

101. Make him a handmade card.

Crystal Brothers

101+ Free/Cheap Date Night Ideas

Funds low? No babysitter? No worries. You can still enjoy some great time with your husband. Here are some great date activities—many are free and don't require a babysitter. Hopefully these ideas will inspire you to get creative and come up with your own additions to the list.

Tip: Copy some of these ideas onto slips of paper and choose one when you need a date idea. The element of surprise makes it even more fun.

Free Date Ideas

1. Have a picnic together.

2. Camp out in the backyard.

3. Have a fun photo shoot together.

4. Play games together.

5. Have a candle-lit dessert date after the kids go to bed.

6. Plan a movie night, complete with boxed candy and popcorn.

7. Make a list of silly and serious questions to spark conversation.

8. Slow dance together in your living room.

9. Volunteer somewhere together.

10. Go for a hike.

11. Go for a bike ride together.

12. Cook a meal together.

13. Look through old pictures or scrapbooks from your dating and early marriage years.

14. Play hide & seek.

15. Have a treasure hunt. Take turns hiding something and drawing your spouse a treasure map or giving clues so they can find it.

16. Go fishing.

17. Play H-O-R-S-E.

18. Look at your old yearbooks together.

19. Work a puzzle.

20. Build a snowman together.

21. Have a snowball fight; make homemade cocoa to warm up.

22. Go sledding together.

23. Pick flowers together.

24. Play Frisbie.

25. Go play on the swing set at a local park.

26. Dye Easter eggs together.

27. Lie on a blanket outside and watch the clouds.

28. Feed the ducks at a local park or lake.

29. Have a water fight.

30. Find a free movies-at-the-park night.

31. Lie on a blanket outside and look at the stars, see if you can find any constellations.

32. Go geocaching.

33. Catch fireflies.

34. Snuggle by the fireplace.

35. Dance in the rain.

36. Make s'mores over a fire.

37. Go to a free local fireworks show.

38. Drive around looking at Christmas lights.

39. Drive in the country to see the beautiful colored leaves in the fall.

40. Fly kites.

41. Try a new food together.

42. Jump in piles of leaves.

43. Carve a pumpkin.

44. Play "hangman" with love notes to one another.

45. Brainstorm ideas and then start a new tradition as a couple.

46. Decorate Christmas cookies.

47. Sit outside and watch a sunset together.

48. Visit a home goods store and plan your dream home, just for fun.

49. Go to a mall and "people-watch" or make up what you think the people might be doing before they came to the mall, or after they leave.

50. Go on a nature walk and have a picnic lunch.

51. Sing songs together by a campfire.

52. Go outside and take turns making shapes out of items like leaves, stones, or twigs, while the other person tries to guess what you are making.

53. Play charades.

54. Play tennis.

55. Get a map and mark places you've been together and places you'd like to go.

56. Plan your "dream vacation."

57. Have breakfast in bed together.

58. Have a blind-folded tasting of random fruits or candies.

59. Play twister.

60. Play photo-booth at home. Get out some props and go crazy with silly photos.

61. Recite your wedding vows back to each other.

62. Date Night Jar: Fill a jar with activities and draw one out. The "surprise" element adds some fun!

63. Play Fact or Fiction. List 2 facts about yourself and 1 that isn't true and see if he can guess which is which. Take turns.

64. Mute a corny show and make up your own dialogue.

65. Have a movie night watching your favorite movies from your childhood.

66. Go window shopping.

67. Have a mini-marshmallow war. You each get 20 marshmallows and aim them from the other side of the kitchen at a cup. See who gets the most in. Or just throw them at each other.

68. Make play-dough sculptures of one another.

69. Take turns humming a song and have your spouse guess what it is.

70. Take turns making up silly dance moves.

Cheap Date Ideas

1. Take a dance class

2. Go to a ballgame

3. Go ice-skating together

4. Visit a local museum or attraction

5. Go to the zoo

6. Go to a local high school play or band concert

7. Go horseback riding

8. Go bowling

9. Hit some balls at a batting cage

10. Train for and run a 5k together

11. Go roller-skating

12. Visit a pumpkin patch

13. Play miniature golf

14. Go to the county fair

15. Hit up some garage sales together

16. Go on a hayride

17. Play games at a local arcade

18. Attend a concert

19. Visit a comedy club

20. Go to a coffee house when they have live music playing

21. See a movie at your local discount movie theatre

22. Visit a local corn maze

23. Go to a local high school sporting event

24. Take an acting class together

25. Visit a local historical site together

26. Go to a drive-in movie

27. Complete a home-improvement project together

28. Go out for dessert (it's cheaper than dinner, and kind of fun to go out later)

29. Go to Goodwill and pick out crazy outfits for each other

30. Have a Nerf gun war

31. Go on a paddle boat ride together

32. Recreate your first date

33. Go on a carriage ride

34. Play paintball

Crystal Brothers

101+ Conversation Starters

These conversation starters make a great activity for date night! Copy some of these questions onto slips of paper. Fold them up and place them in a jar. Take turns drawing out a question for your spouse to answer. Visit my site www.servingjoyfully.com for a printable version of some of my favorite questions.

Faith Questions

1. What is your favorite verse of the bible? Why?

2. If you could ask God one question, what would it be?

3. Who is your favorite person in the Bible (besides Jesus)? Why?

4. Which person in the Bible do you most relate to?

5. What is your biggest struggle in following God's will for your life? (Pray with your spouse about this!)

6. What incident in your life most shaped your faith?

7. In what way should a Christian marriage look different from a non-Christian one?

8. If you could have been present at any Biblical event, what would you choose?

9. Has there been a certain time in your life when you felt especially close to God? What was going on at that time?

Fun Questions

1. If a movie were made of your life, what celebrity would you like to play you?

2. If you could be any animal, what would you be?

3. If you were in a circus, what would your job be?

4. What is your favorite candy?

5. What other country would you most like to visit?

6. What is your favorite cartoon character?

7. If you could have any superpower, what would it be?

8. If you weren't born now, what time period would you most like to live in? (Bonus: Try guessing what time period you would choose for your spouse.)

9. If you could only listen to 1 type of music for the rest of your life, what would it be?

10. What historical event do you wish you could have been a part of?

11. Is there a character from a book or movie that you relate to?

12. If you could trade places with someone else for a day, who would you want to be?

13. What is your favorite holiday? Has it changed since you were a kid?

14. Would you rather live on the beach or in the mountains?

15. If you could learn to do anything, what would it be?

16. If we could drop it all and go do something fun right now, what would you want to do?

17. What would your ideal day be spent doing?

18. If you could relive one day in your life, what would it be?

19. If you could be invisible for a day, what would you do?

20. What is your favorite room in our home? Why?

21. If you could have a different name, what would you want yours to be?

Life Questions

1. If you could go anywhere on vacation, where would it be?

2. If you could live anywhere, where would it be?

3. Name 3 people who have had a positive impact on your life.

4. What are your top 3 goals for your life right now?

5. If you were stranded on an island and could only take 3 possessions with you, what would it be?

6. What is your dream car?

7. What do you want for your children when they grow up?

8. If you could have dinner with one person no longer living, who would it be?

9. What is your favorite childhood memory?

10. What from your childhood would you most like to replicate with your children? What do you most want to avoid?

11. What is your favorite time of day?

12. What is something you would like to change about yourself?

13. If you had $1 million, what would you spend it on?

14. Do you believe in miracles? Why or why not?

15. If you could relive a moment from your past what would it be?

16. If you could get one "do-over" and change something you did in your past, would you? What would you want to change?

17. What was the last movie that made you cry?

18. Do you believe that everything happens for a reason?

19. Describe your dream home.

20. What would you like to do when you retire?

21. What was your favorite thing about visiting your grandparents?

22. If you could do any type of volunteer work—money is no issue—what would you want to do?

23. What did you want to grow up and be when you were a kid?

24. If you could open your own business, what would it be?

25. What is your biggest fear?

26. If money weren't a factor, what hobby would you like to pursue?

27. If it were possible to know when and how you were going to die, would you want to?

28. If you could only be one or the other would you prefer to be smart or attractive? Which quality would you prefer in your spouse?

29. Which family member were you closest to while growing up?

30. What is your biggest pet peeve? Why do you think it bothers you so much?

31. If you could give a message to every person alive, what would you say to them?

32. If there were a public execution, would you watch it?

33. Tell me something that I don't know about you.

34. What would you have to accomplish in order to consider yourself a "success" at the end of your life?

35. If walls could talk, what would ours say? How can we improve what that would be?

36. If you had 1 hour to live, what would you do?

37. If you were guaranteed an honest answer to 3 questions, who and what would you want to ask?

38. What are 5 things you want to do before you die?

39. If you become senile, but could remember 1 hour of your life, what would you want to remember?

40. What do you consider to be your greatest strength? Your greatest weakness?

41. What is the most adventurous thing you've ever done?

42. What is the most important trait that you think a parent should have?

43. What would you most want people to remember about you after you die?

44. What are 5 things you're most thankful for right now?

45. What is one quality you admire most about each of your parents?

46. What is the most thoughtful thing anyone has ever done for you?

47. Who was your favorite teacher? Why?

48. Who were your best friends as a kid? Are you still friends with any of them?

49. What "wrong" against you has been most difficult for you to forgive?

50. What is the best advice anyone ever gave you? The worst?

Couple Questions

1. What is your favorite date we've had together?

2. When did you first realize you were in love with me?

3. When did you first realize you wanted to marry me?

4. What are some of your happiest memories of our life together so far?

5. What would a "perfect date" look like for you?

6. What 3 things do you love most about me? If you're brave: What are 3 things I could work on?

7. What can I do to best support you after a rough day?

8. How can I best pray for you?

9. Do you remember the first time we met?

10. What can I do to make you feel most loved and appreciated?

11. When do you find me most attractive?

12. What clothing item would you like to see me wear more often? Which one would you like to see me throw away and never wear again?

13. Do you believe in love at first sight?

14. What is something you wish I would do more often?

15. What real-life couple do you think has the best relationship? What could we learn from them?

16. If you could change 2 things about our relationship, what would it be?

17. What would you like to do for our next anniversary?

18. What is the best compliment that I could give you?

19. What can I do to make you feel honored and respected? Does this change when we are around other people?

20. What is your funniest memory of our dating days?

21. What is your favorite memory of our dating time?

22. What do you wish I would do more of? Less of?

23. When do you remember seeing me the happiest?

24. Since we have been together, what has been your scariest moment?

25. What made you fall in love with me?

ABOUT THE AUTHOR

Crystal Brothers is a child of God. She is a wife to a handsome forest ranger, and a homeschooling mother to two rambunctious boys. She holds a masters degree in English and is a freelance writer. You can find her work in magazines such as *Thriving Family* and more. She blogs at Serving Joyfully where it is her goal to equip and encourage women to serve God and their families with a joyful spirit.

Made in the USA
Columbia, SC
21 September 2020